Finding Fireflies in Ferns

Kakoli Das

BookLeaf Publishing
India | USA | UK

Presentation by *BookLeaf Publishing*

Web: www.bookleafpub.com

E-mail: info@bookleafpub.com

ISBN: 9789360942397

First edition 2024

DEDICATION

To Reet, Rish, Ridhaan. For everything is for you.

To Maa, Deta. For everything is you.

To Moo. For you are the original reason for me to try and be anything. Always wanted to be your hero.

To the girl with whom I find fireflies.

To the boy who finds mallipoo for me.

To Ruskin, Luca, Maya, Corelone, Jerry, Powali, Bathsheba, Smirnoff, Utterly, Butterly, Pepper, Berrie, Deli, Travolta, Junaki, Zarathasthra, Fredo, Huggy, Lilly, Olive, Bella, Maya Jr, Kara, Zoey, Nemo. And you, too Bono. For you taught me the language of love.

About the Author

"Kakoli. Lost and found. As most of us are. Creator of beautiful things, and beautiful stories – of life and living. Eternally hopeful, unbridled in her experience of life. She lives to experience joy, beauty, and exuberance of life. Nothing more, and nothing less.

And whenever she experiences pain, she converts that into beautiful work of art.

Born in Assam, homed in Bangalore. Kakoli feels the change of season in her beloved homeland, faraway from her home in the city that has adopted her. Forever a questioner of life, Kakoli has changed several identities to currently settle into this identity of a woman who blossoms when she is in rhythm with nature. Or else she withers, shrivels. She homes plants, animals, birds, fish in her home along with three curious caterpillars …err…humans that she is raising.

Her wish for life is to be love….not to love…but be love.

Kakoli has a corporate career of two decades. She is slowly leaning into her love for writing, more and more. She is also slowing down in her life to savor her lingering moments with the people she really loves, doing things that nourish them and her."

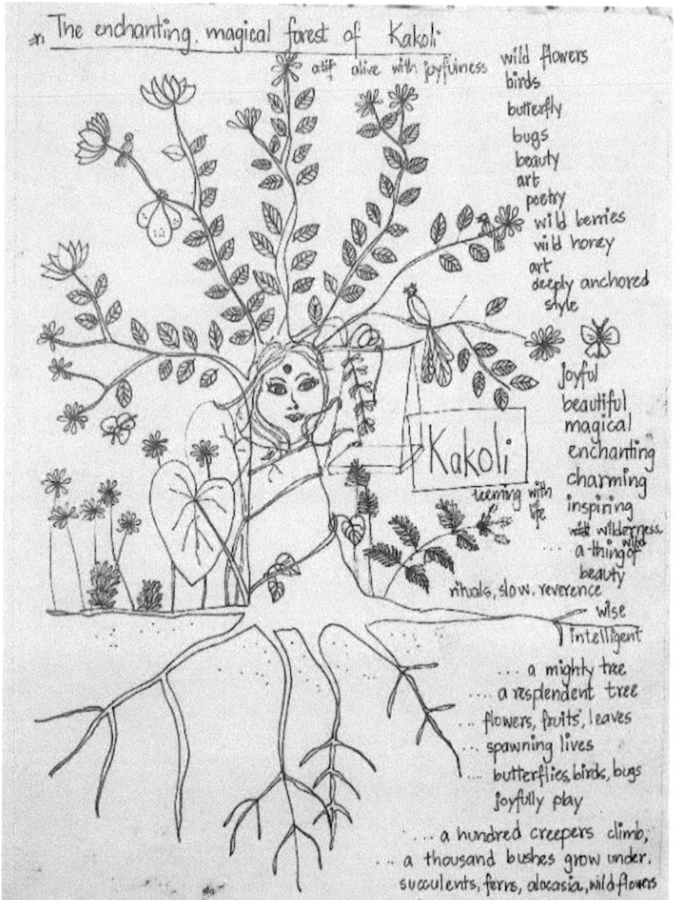

The enchanting, magical forest of Kakoli
alive with joyfulness
wild flowers
birds
butterfly
bugs
beauty
art
poetry
wild berries
wild honey
art
deeply anchored
style
joyful
beautiful
magical
enchanting
charming
inspiring
wilderness.
... a thing of wild beauty
Kakoli
teeming with life
rituals, slow, reverence
wise
intelligent
... a mighty tree
.... a resplendent tree
... flowers, fruits, leaves
... spawning lives
... butterflies, birds, bugs
joyfully play
... a hundred creepers climb,
... a thousand bushes grow under.
succulents, ferns, alocasia, wild flowers
.... a mighty, abundant, resplendent, captivating,
life giving, deeply anchored joyful presence.

ACKNOWLEDGEMENT

Thank you Maa, Deta for raising me to be me. Thank you for tolerating my early existential crisis, and doing whatever you could to support me, even though you did not understand why. You stood by me, always, even when I turned my face away from you. You were always there, watching my back, waiting for me to turn around, so that you could look into my eyes to try and understand my needs. Only so that you could proactively organize whatever I needed at that phase of my life, to find my joy. Be happy, Majoni. Be happy. Find what makes you happy. That's perhaps the shortest parenting book written ever—find what makes you happy, be happy.

Aaah Reet, Rish and Ridhaan! Where do I begin! Thank you for allowing me to grow up again with you, while I raised you. Thank you for unconditionally loving me. Thank you for unconditionally accepting me. Thank you for unconditionally forgiving me. Thank you for that assurance—

"You are the best Mamma in the whole world."
"How did I get so lucky? 8 billion people in the world, and I get you as my Mamma!"
"I love you more than where numbers end"
"The millet pizza base is better, but it's still the best millet pizza base in the world"
Thank you for teaching me motorsports, Kurzgesagt. Minecraft, and about fourteen different types of fart. It is your curiosity that helps me find language for mine.

My dear sister, Nilakshi, for every word of doubt that I had, you replaced that with a positive spin. If not for your timely appearance in my life, and in my days (yes, right around snack time), I would be in negative spirals. You and your fascination for neuroscience helped me recraft myself.

To Tanuj, for being so invested in me to vocalize the angle I should try in between squash shots. The best decisions in my life have happened in the proximity of the sister and you.

To Rekha. If not for you, I would not have found my art. You are my teacher of creativity.

To the Sisterhood of Shaktiship, it's in that safe space I found my art.

To Swati. If not for you, I would never have continued my practice of creating art.

To Saravana. If not for you, I would have remained an author who has published several books in her mind. Doing to my being.

The mighty tree.
The mighty still tree.
The mighty anchored still tree.
The mighty nurturing anchored still tree.
The mighty tree.
Hundred languages.
Thousand possibilities.
The mighty tree.
Thats me.

PREFACE

"Raise your words, not voice. It is rain that grows flowers, not thunder." — Rumi
I still remember that morning when this dawned on me. I was holding my breath in a particular step of a Surya namaskar series, on the verandah of a house named Tulip. That I don't want to be thunder. I don't want to slay. I do not want to slaughter. I do not want to fight.

I want to grow flowers. I want to learn the language of flowerspeak.

I want a life of ease, play, joy.

I started raising my words.

I started weaving words into poems.

The Ship Not on the Shore

Walk slow, they said.
My legs were in sync with my galloping
thoughts.

Think twice, they said.
Life is finite, said my head.

Bite what you can chew, they said.
My heart homed 46 dogs.

Don't rush in love, don't trust, they said.
Save your tears, they said.
Doubt everyone, use caution, they said.

But…
My heart paces in rhythm with my audacity
to dream.

I saw love in the eyes of strangers.
I invited them home.
I marinated Sunday roast.

With an extra dash of wild rockets.
I laid out the precious blue china.

Was I never hurt?
No. No.
I hurt like labor pain.
I birthed a hundred love poems.
I wept till zero visibility.
And….
In between tears….
I played.
I hopped.
I skipped.
I laughed.
I lived.

Metamorphosis : Of Tejimola, Ruskin and Luca

Once therc was a girl.
Her name was Tejimola.
Beautiful.
Graceful.
Charming.
Captivating.
Can't be hidden.
Can't be made oblivious.
Hence,
When her doting father was away,
The step mother pounded her to death.

Then.
She became,
A bottle gourd plant.
A citrus tree.
A lotus flower.
And eventually metamorphosed into…
A squirrel.
To exist in some form.
To engulf her doting father.

With presence.

Once I had two dogs.
Ruskin and Luca.
Beautiful.
Playful.
Vivacious.
Can't be hidden.
Can't be ignored.

One was snatched overnight.
They said he bloated up.
And died alone.
In asphyxiation.

Ruskin struggled.
Torn between love.
For his brother, and
For I.

He barked one day.
His strongest bark.
And left, leaving nothingness.
But ever since,
My terrace garden blossomed.
Butterflies visited.
Moths made homes.

Guppies spawned.
Budgerigars came home.
I spotted fireflies,
During my walks in the dusk.

Metamorphosis??

Precision of Predictive Analytics

There is charm,
Of long-distance love,
Of network drops,
And phone calls with lag.

Of finding your way,
Through the maze,
Of time zones.
Of planning for months,
To meet for a handful,
In days.

But.
Have you wondered…
Of the joy of precision of predictive analytics,
When the girl you love,
Lives in your neighborhood?

She sees the sun rise,
As you do.
She sees the full moon,
The same fraction of time,

When your WhatsApp message
Announces that black clouds have pulled away,
With the pic you clicked in night mode.
Words and language can be dropped,
They seem like overhead.
For there is synchronicity,
Of space, and time.

And you know exactly,
To time a Swiggy delivery.
Of samosas, fresh and warm,
To accompany her freshly brewed tea.

For you know,
She, a lover.
Of rains and Assam team.
And that, as soon as the clouds rumble,
In your corner of the world,
Her hands would stretch,
For a pot of tea,
And that she would spin stories,
In between sips.
It's a privilege of relativity of time.
When the girl you love,
Lives in your neighborhood.

The Pandemic Child

I am Ridhaan.
I am 7.
I feel like 5.
Because I celebrated only 5 birthdays.

What is school?
A screen that opens up when I click a blue line called Zoom on my laptop.

What is Zoom?
A word I learnt before I could learn Jolly Phonics.

What is life?
Life is what happens on my laptop.
Stories, music, and even sports.
And life is good when I am the host of a Zoom meeting.
Then I can mute everyone, and do as I please.

What is freedom?
Is basically if I can unmute myself or not.

Who is a friend?
Someone whose parent's phone number is
stored on my mother's phone.
And I have permission to call.
When my mother is not working.

What is learning?
Some sheets that I need to take photos of,
and upload on Google drive.
Learning creates stress for my mother.
Because she is tired at the end of the day,
And is confused.
Between the Google drives of Reet, Rish
and Ridhaan.

What is home?
A place where I always find Mamma.
Mostly on her Microsoft Teams calls.
But she's home.
Always.

The Sibling in a Child of Mine

I have a sister.
I also have a child who reminds me of the sister.
It's like a tiny part of her has found its way into this child of mine,
Regrowing.
Another feisty chance at life's mischief,
And adventures.
Which are still within the realm of possibilities of the child.
In the sparkling eyes.
In his never-ending imagination.
In his million experimentations,
Of dismantling everything functional in the house.
Most of all,
In his deep sense of alignment within.
He is centered, in him.
Just like she is, in her.

The Tempest of Thoughts : When the Future Meets the Present

Today, I woke up different.

I remember sleeping early last night,
My head hurting from something unexplained.
Waves of thoughts rummaging and boomeranging,
Some on the verge of gaining escape velocity,
Breaking free from my headspace.
Whilst some others pulled towards the center,
Under the influence of an invisible centripetal force.
Making my core dense.
And firm.
Changing the state of my core.
Steady state from excited, random Brownian motion.

I could see this cauldron inside my head, on fire.
Brimming with bubbling thoughts.
Some gaining a sudden sense of belonging to me,
And settling down.
And some evaporating, escaping.

The war of the unfamiliar and the familiar.
Resulting in an all-new concoction.

I remember telling my amused child:
I am becoming a butterfly from a caterpillar.

Today, I woke up different.
Today, the future met the present:
A caterpillar woke up a butterfly.

Colorful Beanies and the Joyous Moments of Hopelessness

Colorful beanies transport me to Kate
Winslet's dreams.
In Eternal Sunshine of the Spotless Mind.
To Pink Floyd,
And wish you were here.

Hopeless romantic?
There's so much hope in this hopelessness.
So much hope.

Life often becomes utilitarian,
Shriveled and withered.
Barren.
These moments of hopelessness are like the
heady April showers.
Where love and poetry
Make a beanstalk out of the oak tree,
Flexible and fluid out of rigid.
Softness from hardened.
And the avalanche of magic

Bulldozes the strong will to make meaning.
Make sense.
Make logic.
Make it count.

It's in the dearth of the moments of
hopelessness,
That hope is lost.

I am a hopeless romantic.
Colourful beanies,
Kate Winslet,
Jim Carret.
Pink Floyd,
Eternal Sunshine of Spotless Mind.
Make me very, very happy.

Teaching Myself to Give Birth to Me: An Ode to Menstrual Pain and PMS

The crescent moon reminds me,
Labour pain has been induced.
Treacherous,
Screaming for attention,
Unbearable pain of birthing.

I can no longer ignore,
The needy being inside me.

It needs love, that I have deprived.
It needs care, that I have compromised.
It needs rest, that I have denied.

It needs fuel for dreams, that I have dishonored.
It throws tantrums, like a gush of unstoppable wind.
It spews anger,
When not heard,
When the flame is not fanned.

It becomes ugly, messy, unapologetic,
chaotic, unignorable.
It becomes:
the completely expressed,
the unsuppressed,
Me.

Then someday it's full moon,
And I birth ME,
Incrementally.
One lunar cycle after another.

Botanical Voyeurism

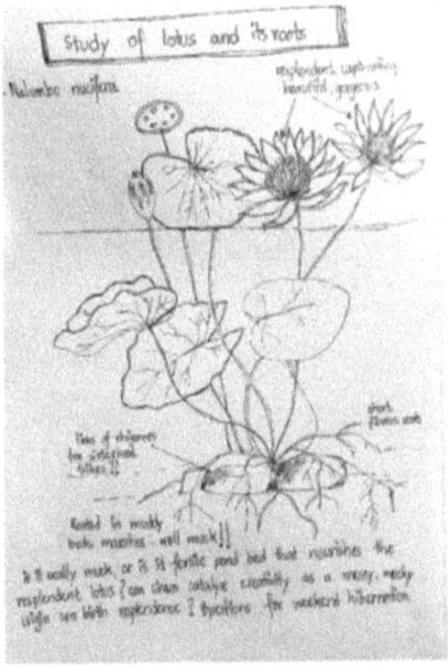

Peeping tom of balconies,
And windowsills,
I indulge in voyeuristic pleasure,
Every day early morning.
When balconies are deserted,
And birds have not yet perched on
windowsills.

I fantasize about human hands,
And souls,
That nourished the lush green.

Or.

Of the grief that passed through households,

Resulting in withered, abandoned balconies.
Once alive,
And now a heap of dead leaves.

The Gateway to Heavenly Delight

I can see beautiful things.
That's my gift.

I can see a verandah surrounded by pink
bougainvillea.
And madhobi lota foliage metamorphosed
into a graceful arch.
I can see cane chairs.
And vintage teapot, cosy with a
cross-stitched tea cozy.
I can feel winter sun rays too.
Crepescular.
Komorebi.
And its warmth on my
oil-soaked-ten-year-old self.
Peeling oranges into snakes.

I can weave a beautiful love story.
I can hear Rumi being read, and
experienced,
In my curling toes, and my gushing
bloodstream.

I can see a picnic table.
And noisy, happy children playing frisbee.
And shiny, happy people holding hands.
I can see boisterous dogs, and bubbles.
And rows and rows of lavendars,
Not in an arrangement,
But bustling with life and wilderness.

I can hear laughter, of friends.
I can hear Tagore being recited.

All of these through “the gate to heavenly delights”:
Translucent and see-through.
Everything is visible.
But.
Guarded by the ghost,
Who feeds on the memory of ugly past,
Who I can’t get past,
To access the heavenly delights.

Finding Purpose

There are levels of finding purpose.
Sometimes we look at the highest possible expression,
And tell ourselves,
I can be that too.

A Marjane Satrapi.
An Amelia Earhart.
Or Anoushka Shankar.
Or Nikita Gill.

And that serves.
Only till the extent it serves no more.

For something inside tugs.
Imagine.
If Ada Lovelace emulated someone who has already been created,
And available for reference in history books?
Or Simone De Beauvoir, or Maya Angelou, or Ayn Rand?

There would be no Second Sex, or
Phenomenal Woman, Or Atlas Shrugged.

Finding purpose is then to find you.
Without the constraints of the scaffolding of an archetype.
Or the floors and ceilings of benchmarks.

Who would you be—
even if there are no hands to clap for your stellar performance?
Even if the world, in its present, did not need you?

At the end of this shifting,
Through the sieve of connectedness to the sense of self,
A path emerges,
To "finding purpose".

We are all waves of the ocean of creation.
But we have our unique quirk.
Our own dance.

Bottleneck of De-clutter

Some mornings,
When you wake up at the crack of dawn,
And let the breeze come in,
The morning breeze that has secrets to tell.

You know it's time.
It's time to clean up the mess.
Declutter.

That old photo album that was never used.
The bottles of capsules and medicines,
That probably could have been required
some midnight.
But were never required in the past 6 years.

The unused pens.
The leftover pasta of various shapes.
That plant that has died six months ago,
And the stained pot that holds its dead parts
together.

The dog's stained bed.
The many useless plastics.

Someday you have got to throw it all.
To make space.

Beauty is a real-life pursuit.
Space needs to be created for beauty.
In the shelves of the mind.

And if gathering clutter is justifying the procrastination,
Well,
The world has forgiven you,
Only your forgiveness is the bottleneck.

Butterflies on a Gulmohar Tree

Love meets as butterflies.
Each eager to show the other,
Treasures and troves and patches of charcoal
black dappled with pink.
"So much beauty that I discovered,
Secrets well-kept.
I now want to share all that's precious,
With you,"
The butterflies seem to say.

Then love grows roots.
It dreams of becoming a Gulmohar tree.
Nestled by a rock,
And a seasonal spring.

Love wants to become stable and sturdy.
And deep-rooted.
Love dreams of a mighty foliage,
The flamboyance of a Gulmohar tree.

Love still wants butterflies.
But wants to home them instead.
Butterflies on a Gulmohar tree.

The Date with Moi

I take myself on a date.
And asked, beloved—what do you seek?

Flowers. Flowers. Flowers.
To play with them.
To adorn them.
To adorn myself with them.
To make flower art.
And preserve the fragrance of memories of moments,
In between the pages of my hardbound
Alice in Wonderland.

Wilderness.
To play with gushing streams.
To watch the silly salmon swim upstream, and glee.
There will be pebbles, moss ferns.
I will gather them in a mason jar.
And place it by the windowsill.

A rustic kitchen with access to a vegetable garden.

To cook.
To experiment.
To create an alchemy of love, deep care and delight.

Maximalist library.
Lined with books that reek of old times, and some as fresh as new.
To understand Fibonacci and Newton.
Leo Tolstoy and Satrapi.
And draw parallels between Einstein and Vedic Astrology.
To understand speed and relativity.
To understand the geometry of the universe.
And how energy flows through crests and troughs,
Sometimes as ecstasy.
And sometimes as catastrophe.

A craft room. Just as the one I saw in Bothell.
Needles. Yarns. Canvas. Paints. Trinkets.
Abundance of space.
Undisturbed blocks of time.
To sew monograms on handkerchiefs.
To make pretty things.

But.
Most of all.
To keep this heart a magical place.
Of beauty, love and devotion.

Falling in Love, is a Way to Me

Falling in love, to me
Is an indication…….
I have found a path,
Which could lead me to me.

Because how can I love
What I see in the reflection
If I already not
Recognize it as my own?

Falling in love
To me
Is an indication.
I have found a way
To the maze of me.

268 Lines of MVP

The earth gets 365 and a quarter.
The moon can ebb and flow in 28 through her many moods.
Pluto of course is vacationing.
How else do you explain the time expanse of 268 years?

But I get only 7, and 7 days only?
Eat, aspire, despair.
And repeat?
Hard boot. Reset.
In chunks of 24 hrs?

- Wednesdays are for love, and tea.

And bandaging and repairing of my heart.

- Thursdays I am an amazon.

Rekindled zeal of a repaired heart.

- Fridays are for a witches' meet.

We gather around a fire.
Design and experiment the concoction of a magic spell,

To heal the entire Milky Way, and perhaps aim for the universe.

- Saturdays I open school bags.
To account for missing spoons, forks, and lids of fruit boxes.
And who knows, discover bugs and stones and sticks?
Safely tucked in crevices.

- Sundays are for homemade soaps of oats, banana and honey,
And warm olive oil massages.
But I mostly daydream.

- Mondays I pretend I have memory loss.
And convince the people around me that I woke up on Sunday.

- Tuesdays I draw up a list of things that bring me joy.
Can I live on Pluto instead?
I have enough to fill 268 X 365 line items on an excel sheet.
But okay, I will negotiate.
I will contain my effervescence.

I will just take two sixty.
(And eight for some space for pixie dust)
That will be my MVP.
Minimum Viable Product of Me.

To All the People I Will Never Meet

To all the people who I never met.
To all the people who I will never meet.

Were you staring at online content buffering when I passed by?
Were you lamenting decisions made in the past,
While I just showed up in your present?

Were you languishing?
Were you mourning?
Were you oblivious?

How could it be that I am alive,
And so are you,
And yet we did not meet.

To all the people who I will never meet,
Will you commit to be born again?
Live another life?
And this time, meet me?
Be a collision of synchronicity?

Nostalgia of Familiarity

I woke up with myriad thoughts:
Foggy mornings,
A certain home in Assam,
A certain little girl I call sister,
A father snug in a shawl,
Handwoven with hand-spun eri;
Which were reared in his mother's
backyard.
A mother hustling bustling,
In a hand-knitted sweater,
Busy serving hot things to keep the family
warm.

Raag Bhairav comes to my mind:
A harmonium.
A taanpura.
And two little girls in morning riyaaz,
Sulking in defiance:
They don't get the point
Why Bhairav with its flat notes
Has to be sung at the crack of dawn.

Over the years,

I have distanced myself,
From the home,
From the people,
From those sights and sounds,
As if escaping the familiar
Will give flight to my dreams,
Which were unfamiliar in that small house
in a small town,
We called home.

My efforts were in escaping.
As if my familiar will trap me.
But today,
In the autumn of my life,
I know the familiar anchors me.

That home.
Mother. Father. Raag Bhairav.
Assam.
Quiet study time in the evenings.
Sharing that space under a mosquito net
with the sister.

My audacious dreams take root,
In the safety and stability of my familiar.

Gratitude to Summer

There is something about the onset of
summer.
There's something about the heaviness of
the cold winter mornings lifting up,
Making way for the sweltering sun....

It is not a burden yet,
Not yet the merciless, overpowering sun.

It is a sign of shifts,
Of transitions.
Of one phase to the other.

Almost like these flaming, hungry waves of
hopes of newness,
Are on a rush,
To lure you in,
And perhaps devour you later.

That's for another day, another time,
When I will whine,
Complain of dying of the cold apathy of the
scorching sun.

But today,
I will see the brightness as hope.

And will daydream of :

Ripe and fat Baiganpalli and the cool kosamari,
The pink of the watermelon wedges against the bottle green.
Vidya's garden and the shady shelter of the fig tree.
Shaher's terrace and the mango branches,
Bending with the bounty of the fruits it's bearing.
Summer paddle pool parties,
And bubble guns and yellow duckies.

And of our efforts of building a community garden,
And the book, "Farm in a pot", from the neighborhood library.

Of many mommy friends reading books from the curation,
Neatly organized in a wicker basket.
Taking turns,
Assuring each other—

The world can rush to get somewhere,
We can take our time to linger,
And raise,
Fine human beings.

Thank you, summer.
With you, I re-created childhood memories.

Deep-rooted Beauty

Beauty is skin deep.
Really?

It's not what I wear.
It's the time I spend to intentionally pick up an outfit.

Some things draw me.
Some things don't.

Not having the choice:
Of time,
Of that freedom to choose,
Is poverty of life.

And having is not opulence.
It's access to create beauty.

It's not an array of skin care products.
It's a ritual.
A sacred one.
It's a mindset that I matter.
It's valuing me enough to care for me.

Every inch of me.

Every time I hear beauty is skin deep,
I think again.

Can there be resplendent foliage without
deep roots:
Designed intentionally to nourish?

Beauty is more than skin deep.

It’s in the thought of drying eucalyptus
leaves from the cut flower vase,
To adorn a gift tag for someone I love for
some time in the future.

Beauty is intentionality.
And I crave beauty.

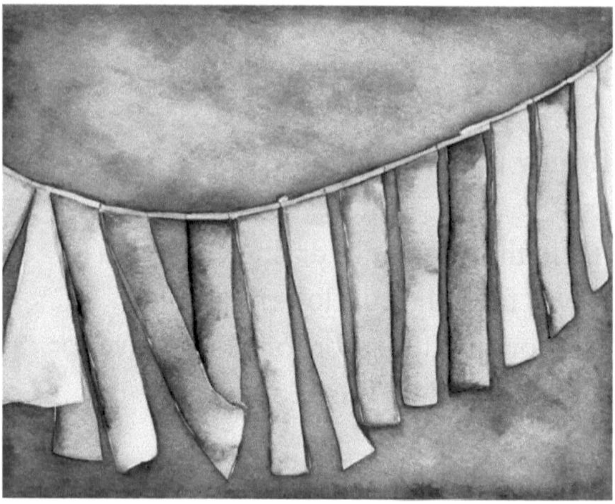

The Hibiscus Whispers

There are some days,
When I become the medium.

The pen moves.
Twists and turns to make marks.
Which I later learned to decipher.
As words.

The words become a mere conduit.
For beauty, love and devotion,
Which have homed my heart.

Prayer flags flutter.
Even if they are adorning an urban balcony.
They whisper prayers in my heart.
"Wake up at dawn, bow your head with
gratitude.
Shower first of course. Shed those layers of
yesterday.
Of doubt. And cynicism. And fixed points of
view.
And pray for the peace of everyone.
May we become ripples of love."

And I listen to the flutter.
I thank the prayer flags.

I feel cleansed. Fresh. New.
I have taken out Persepolis, Rupi Kaur, tarot decks.
And my several packs of micro-tip pens.
I clean the altar.
I readjust the images.
I remember what matters.
Flower mandalas, conch shells and poetry.
And the pressed hibiscus collected from a walk some time ago.
The same walk when I found fireflies in ferns.

I withdraw from the world.
I let it go, dissolve peacefully.
For I have found everything I seek, within.
Love flows.
Peace envelopes.
Words become poems.
Lines become art.
I become one with the world.
Everything becomes me.

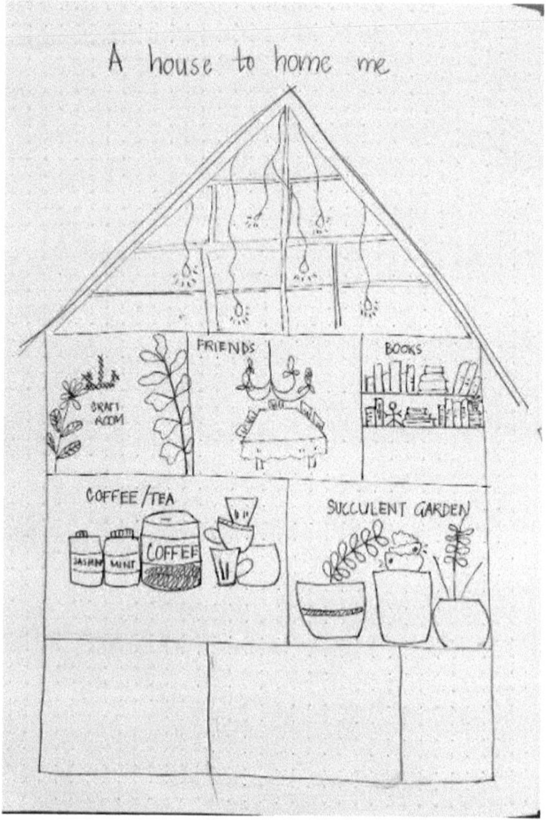

A house to home me
FRIENDS
BOOKS
CRAFT ROOM
COFFEE/TEA
SUCCULENT GARDEN
MINT
COFFEE

Home Sanctuary

Sink full of dishes
While three babies need their mom
Time slips through wet hands
Dust gathers freely
In corners where dreams once bloomed

Dead plants tell stories
Pinterest perfect homes
Mock from my phone screen at night

Reality bites
Lavender longings
Fresh linens remain folded
In imagination

Garden thyme withers
While milk spills and tears flow fast
Both need attending

Chaos multiplies
Like laundry piles reaching high

Peace stays out of reach
Picture-perfect life

Trapped behind smudged windowpanes
Just beyond my grasp
In this messy space
Three hearts beat close to my own

Love grows anyway
Sacred sanctuary
Lives somewhere in tomorrow
Today, we survive.

The Clock Hands Dance

Between whistles and wickets, and
controllers that click,
Three voices rise up in a chorus of "Pick
Me first!" "No, it's my turn!" "Mom, he's not
being fair!"
While I referee life from my worn kitchen
chair.

In stolen moments between matches and
drives,
I glimpse another woman, one who thrives
In spaces where sunlight catches ceramic
glaze,
Where artisanal coffee perfumes lazy days.
She wears dragonfly wings that dance at her
ears,
Her high-waisted belt catches light as she
steers
Through galleries and studios with confident
grace,
Perfect denim hugging curves in all the right
place.

But the clock hands spin faster, calendar pages fly,
Reality breaks through my dream with its cry:
"The meeting! The project! The deadline's at nine!"
No time to search through Lego mines

For that lip gloss, I bought in a moment of hope
When I thought I could somehow learn to cope
With being both women—the dreamer, the doer,
The one who pays bills and the one who's newer.

So I twist up my hair in its messy crown,
Pull on track pants that have seen half the town,
Rush out the door with my laptop in hand,
To earn what it takes to keep life's demands:

The football, the cricket, the Xbox games,
The classes that hopefully justify claims
That someday these boys will grow to be

The kind of men who'll make space for both
she's:

The mother who juggles their world with
care,
And the woman who dreams of dragonflies
in her hair.
For now, I'll dance to the clock's stern song,
Knowing somehow that before too long,

These days of chaos will softly fade,
But the love in this juggling act will stay.

July in Red

I never knew red could be a revolution
until that July when I declared my evolution.
Thirty-one days of defiance, painted in
shades
that refused to fade like my motherhood
days.

Behind diapers and schedules, I'd
disappeared—
a ghost of myself, just as I'd feared.
But red, oh red, has always been
the color of women who refused to be
unseen.

I studied its history like the nerd I am:
how red lips once marked women as
damned,
how flappers and suffragettes wore it with
pride,
how even in wartime, this color defied.

Now names like poetry roll off my tongue:

Rouge Dior (my first), when the journey began,
Stila's Stay All Day (outlasts coffee and kisses),
One Hot Mess (perfectly named, but never misses).

Time Traveler's Muse whispers tales of before,
Ruby Woo promises what's still in store.
Chambor Riot—oh how aptly named!
For the riot in my heart can't be tamed.

I fill boards with images of women who dared:
Alexandria's fierce smile, perfectly flared
in confident crimson; Katherine's classic grace;
Marilyn's power to command time and space.

Each morning in July, I arm myself anew,
studying my reflection—is this really true?
This woman emerging from years of fade,
claiming her space in each shade?

My children watch, curious at first,

then accepting—as if they always knew
their mother contained multitudes of red:
fierce love, bold dreams, and this:
the simple courage to be seen.

In the mirror, I practice my smile,
red-lipped and growing bolder by the mile.
Some days it feels like costume, like play,
until I realize—that's exactly the way

we find ourselves: in small rebellions,
in careful studies of brave hellions,
in thirty-one days of choosing red,
in all the books and blogs I've read.

For in each swipe of crimson bold,
I'm writing stories yet untold.
Not just mother, not just wife,
but woman claiming her own life.

July may end, but this red will stay—
my battle cry, my right to say:
I am here, I choose to shine,
in all these shades of red divine.

Becoming Pippy at 40

At forty, my pin-up girl isn't Marilyn or Audrey—it's a freckle-faced redhead with gravity-defying pigtails and mismatched socks. While other women might have vision boards filled with elegant cocktail dresses and Mediterranean villas, I stand before my bathroom mirror at 5 AM, attempting to defy both gravity and middle-age propriety with my hair.

"Thing-finder," I whisper to my reflection, trying on Pippi's confidence like a borrowed dress that might just fit if I stand straight enough.

Oh, Pippi Longstocking, you magnificent chaos agent! While I'm here counting calories and worrying about my 401(k), you're somewhere lifting horses with one hand and making pancakes on your belly. You never fretted about whether your clothes sparked joy or if your lifestyle choices were Pinterest-worthy. You just lived, horizontal braids flying in the wind, a walking rebellion against every "should" that ever "shoulded."

Every morning, before the house wakes and demands its tribute of packed lunches and signed permission slips, I practice my Pippi-isms. "I have never tried that before, so I think I should definitely be able to do that," I declare to the toothpaste-speckled mirror, while my sensible cotton pajamas judge me silently. Sometimes, I put on my daughter's striped knee socks under my work slacks—my secret act of Pippi solidarity.

The thing about Pippi is she never apologized for taking up space. She never started sentences with "I'm sorry, but..." or ended them with "...if that's okay with everyone?" She lived in Villa Villekulla with a horse on her porch and a monkey for company, and not once did she worry about what the property values were doing to the neighborhood. At forty, I'm still learning to stop apologizing for entering rooms.

Mallipoo Meditations

Dawn's gentle whisper
White petals in waiting rows
My fingers remember
Death metal screams loud
While mallipoo scents my hair
Both rhythms are mine
"Choose sides," they tell me
As if joy must have borders
My heart knows better
Between feminist
And feminine, I create
My own sacred space
Bindis and bangles
Dance with my faded blue jeans
No contradiction
Time bends and yields here
As I thread each jasmine bloom
My rebellion blooms
They see submission
I feel liberation's touch
In each white petal
What box can contain
Both thorns and temple flowers?

I overflow all
Morning ritual:
Adorning myself with time
That the world won't give
My hair carries now
Generations of women
Who chose their own way
Mallipoo crowns me
Not for them, but for myself
My grace, my power
Between then and now
Between their rules and my truth
Mallipoo finds its home

Alchemy of afternoon tea

Across city streams of concrete and steel,
she travels to this moment of porcelain
revelation.
Two hours by metro, thirty minutes by bus,
all for this: her friend's hands dancing
over tea leaves like a conductor before an
orchestra.

Each measure precise as prayer:
darjeeling dreams weighed to the gram,
water heated to exactly ninety-five—
not boiling, never rushing,
patience is the secret ingredient
in this laboratory of joy.

The golden-rimmed cups wait,
white as fresh linen,
pink roses caught in eternal bloom
around their delicate waists.
They've seen a thousand conversations,
held secrets like honey at their bottom.

She works her magic, this tea-witch,

this keeper of sacred proportions,
letting leaves unfurl their stories
in water clear as morning.

Three minutes, forty-five seconds:
timing is everything in love and tea.

A golden spoon rests unopened
to its destiny beside the sugar bowl—
they know better than to alter
this perfect alchemy of leaf and time.

Marble cake stands guard, swirled
with the same precision as the tea.

Two women at a table:
to the world, perhaps, a simple scene.
But here, between the pouring
and the first shared sip,
universes align, stars pause
in their ancient dance to watch.

This is their temple:
gold-rimmed cups, rising steam,
the way afternoon light catches
in the amber tide of perfect tea.
Time dissolves like sugar

they'll never need to add.

In this moment, they are ageless:
priestesses of an ancient ritual,
modern-day enchantresses
who know that magic lives
in measured leaves, timed steeps,
and friendships that travel hours
just to share a perfect cup.

So they sip, these sisters of the leaf,
while the city spins madly beyond their
walls.
Here, in this sanctum of steam and story,
they've found what temples always
promised:
transcendence in the ordinary,
divinity in the daily,
infinity in a teacup.

Summers in Vidya's Garden

In her garden, time ripens differently—
slow as honey dripping from summer's
spoon,
sweet as the jacaranda's purple rain,
wild as the gulmohar's fiery plumes.

Children from Moyenville, Wellington,
Eagle, and Setlur
find their way here like homing birds,
while others chase structured summers
in camps with printed schedules and
measured worth.
Here, there are no schedules to keep,
only the sun's lazy arc marking our days.

The teepee stands sentinel,
keeper of whispered secrets and afternoon
dreams,
while the tire swing writes circles in the air,
collecting children's laughter in its orbit.

Up in the treehouse, young explorers
map territories of imagination,
under branches that remember

other summers, other children,
other stories held in their bark.

Mothers spread themselves across picnic rugs,
bodies soft and unguarded as summer clouds,
wearing their curves like medals of honor—
these vessels that carried the same children
now shrieking through garden hose rainbows,
splashing in blue inflatable seas.
No one here needs to hide
the geography of motherhood
mapped across their skin.

Watermelon slices smile red and sweet,
juice running down small chins.
Mangoes, golden as the afternoon light,
leave their sticky blessing on fingertips.
Potato wedges appear like magic,
and homemade sliders vanish just as quick,
while stories flow between bites,
between breaths, between being.

We take turns, we mothers,
voices rising and falling with story rhythms,

puppet shows emerge from borrowed socks
and scraps of dreams.
Our hands remember how to plant,
how to create, how to hold space
for this precious pause.

Here in Vidya's garden,
rest is not a luxury to be earned
but a birthright to be claimed.
While the world spins faster,
demanding more, more, more,
we rebel with our stillness,
our gentle gathering,
our unhurried joy.

Summer after summer,
the garden holds us all:
the trees that guard our peace,
the grass that cushions our dreams,
the flowers that mark our seasons,
the children who grow like wild things,
the mothers who remember how to rest,
and Vidya, keeper of this sacred space
where time still knows how to pause,
where belonging needs no name,
where summer still tastes
like freedom.

Finding Fireflies in Ferns

Two girls wandering without destination,
their hearts full of half-formed dreams,
step into evening's gentle dissolution
where suburban streets unravel at their
seams.

Between manicured lawns and measured
lives,
where fitness trackers count steps like coins,
they find an untamed patch of earth that
thrives
where two proud villas fail to join.

Others pass by, eyes fixed on glowing
screens,
counting steps toward promised health,
missing how the dusk transforms and leans
into a different kind of wealth.

Then—
Oh then!

The ferns ignite with living stars,
fireflies rising like answered prayers,

each pulse of light, a reminder that
magic still lives between the layers
of ordinary days.

These same girls who pause for moss
spreading emerald tales on stone,
who read the stories of time's gloss
in bark where years have grown,
Who lie in grass to watch clouds bloom
into creatures yet unnamed,
find worlds within a mushroom's room
and joy in things untamed.

While others chase their happiness
in places clearly marked,
these girls know bliss lives best
in spaces wild and dark,
in moments unplanned and free,
in corners left to grow,
in learning how to see
what others never know.

For life's most precious gifts arrive
not when we hunt them down,
but when we learn to stay alive
to wonder's silent crown.

Like now, in this unplanned hour,
when magic shows its face
to those who hold the power
to pause in nature's grace.

And years from now, they'll still recall
this lesson soft and stern:
that greatest joys of all
come finding fireflies in ferns.

Majoni's Dawn

Little Majoni knows the secret:
dawn belongs to falling stars—
white xewali stars that drift
from branches in the dark.

At four years old she learned to wake
before the tree could shake
its blossoms to the waiting earth,
before the morning's break.

Wrapped in grandmother's knitted love,
wool bonnet, sweater warm,
she gathers nature's quiet gifts
while darkness slowly transforms.

One by one she fills her basket,
patient as the stars,
hundreds of white petals blessed
by morning's silver hours.

To mother's hands, she offers them,
these pieces of the dawn,
while garden birds still dream in nests
and dew pearls grace the lawn.

Four decades pass like morning mist,
yet still at four she wakes—
xewali's gift now roots so deep
no morning habit breaks.

In this hushed hour before the world
remembers how to rush,
her dreams speak clear as falling flowers
in autumn morning's hush.

Still gathering gifts, though different now:
inspiration's gentle rain,
while somewhere in her garden heart
that small girl stays the same—

Forever reaching for white stars
that fall from xewali trees,
forever wrapped in morning's peace,
forever wild and free.

Beauty
Fibbnacci
Fibonacci
LOVE golden ratio
floriographist
sunflower
There seems to be this notion...
...there can be....
— Poetry "or" prose.
— Vivid imagination "or" stable predictabili
– wilderness of a blossomed woman "or" safe haven of a homing wife.
– style "or" comfort
– romantic lover "or" doting mother
– ambitions "or" a loving, nurturing family
– success "or" of conscious choices.
–making money "or" a beautiful home.
mostly, ethereal beauty "or" earthly wisdom.
science "or" spirituality
art "or" intelligence
tradition "or" progress.
I DEFY THAT STATUS QUO

The Girl Who Refused to Choose

At six, she knew the secrets
of how to fold a prawn roll just so –
crisp edges, golden dreams,
surprise hidden in every bite.

While other children played with toys,
she played with possibility:
pine cones became centerpieces,
rocks transformed into paperweights,
each flower foraged told a story
of beauty found, not bought.

Her mother's women's magazines in
Bengali whispered their wisdom
to her eager eyes:
how to make a house sing,
how to turn ordinary moments
into small celebrations.

At five, she crowned egg curry
with cilantro wreaths and green chilli stars,
while quantum physics danced

in her daydreams,
and mathematics wrote love letters
in her margins.

They told her she must choose:
theorems or tea leaves,
equations or embroidery,
academic halls or kitchen walls.
As if her heart could not hold
both kinds of beautiful.

But she dreamed in multiple dimensions:
of freshly laundered sheets
catching constellations in their folds,
of serving warm meals
while discussing warm quarks,
of arranging flowers
while rearranging universe theories.

In her world, there was no "or"—
only "and":
Home and hypothesis,
Comfort and calculation,
Nurture and nuclear physics,
Beauty and bold research.

Let them call it audacious, big and hairy
audacious,
this stubborn refusal to divide
her soul into acceptable pieces.
She knows that some equations
can only be solved
by adding, never subtracting:

A house plus a laboratory,
A kitchen plus a classroom,
A heart big enough to hold
All the ways there are
To make this world more beautiful

Where exactly is this so-called busy-ness?

Time flows like water
My mind races ahead fast
While leaves drift slowly
Clock ticks steadily
But thoughts sprint and tumble past
Nature keeps her pace
Racing thoughts create
Storms in cloudless summer skies—
The chaos within

Twenty-four hours
Neither stretch nor shrink their truth
Mind weaves the hurry
Rest becomes hostile
When peace is held hostage by
Self-made urgency.

Living Life on 24hrs a Day

I discovered a treasure trove—a secret of
time I didn't know
Twenty-four brand new hours every day!
Not a single one borrowed from tomorrow
Not a single one stolen from yesterday

What if we spent them like precious
Monopoly money?
Each hour with its own intentional purpose:
Some for dancing with morning shadows
Some for counting stars at night

Could we squeeze in both giggles and
galaxies?
Between breakfast and bedtime's gentle call
Could we find time to climb a mountain
And also watch a raindrop fall?

Could we make a Sharktank pitch
And admire Monet's lilies and pause?

They say time is a scarcity, but I wonder...
Is it, or do we spend it away, inattentively?

Always reaching for tomorrow's promises
While today's possibilities slip away

What if we, that's all we had—24hrs a day,
And you are on a challenge
To win this anyway?

Could we learn to be both
The turtle and the hare?
Racing with passion through moments
While staying perfectly still to care?

Twenty-four hours...
No more, no less
Could this be not our limit
But our daily project of vivaciousness?

I'm learning this strange arithmetic
Where less somehow equals more
When we stop borrowing from tomorrow
Today grows from twenty-four to infinite!

So, here's my wonder-filled question
As we spin round the sun:
What if we mastered this art
Of living each day like our only one?

Not as a sprint or a marathon
But a dance of now and here
Twenty-four hours, fresh every morning
To make life extraordinarily dear!

"Amrapali Speaks"

Yellow walls whisper stories I've dreamed since childhood,
Portuguese arches frame the woman I am becoming.
Like me, and her, this house keeps its secrets in plain sight,
A manifesto of beauty that needed no shouting.

Her Lucknow lives in that salvaged haveli door,
Its wood remembering hands that carved their desires.
And those brass engraved handles from her girlhood home—
How many times did her small fingers trace their edges?

Lucknowi chikan work adorns the glass panes now,
Block-printed papers tell tales of artisan nights.

Each morning light creates new patterns through them,
Like thoughts crystallizing into desires fulfilled.

Paulomi's beauty and Kamakshi's grace
Hold court in her chamber, their canvas eyes knowing
Every dream she has whispered into dawn,
Every vision she is carefully bringing to life.

Gold-rimmed porcelain catches afternoon light,
Each cup holding space for future celebrations.
Her books stand sentinel, spines straight and proud,
Housing worlds within worlds, like this home houses her, and now me.

In the herb garden, basil leaves dance with mint,
Their fragrance rising like answered prayers.
This house, my Amrapali, teaches me daily
That abundance flows from attending to beauty.

She created you, Amrapali,
But, did I create you or did you create me?
Each carefully chosen piece mirrors back
The woman who dared to build her dreams
Into walls and windows, into home and
sanctuary.

Sometimes I pause in your doorway, amazed
At how perfectly you wear my heart's
desires.
Standing here, I understand at last—
This is how abundance feels when it comes
home to stay.

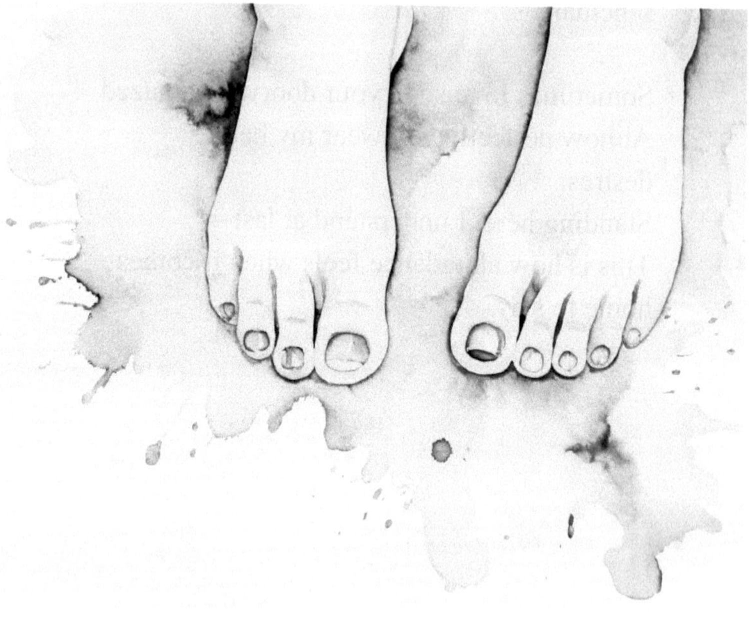

Stories that Feet Tell:

They carry dreams without complaint,
these humble ambassadors of intention—
mapped with lines deeper than palm readers know,
each crack and callus a story of paths chosen.

In winter, they tell truths first:
neglected soles crack like forgotten promises,
while those bathed in oils and attention
bloom even in December's cold.

Some feet speak of rushed mornings,
of battles with time and forgotten grace,
their dry edges whispering of shortcuts taken,
of journeys measured only in arrival.

But then there are those that know love—
rounded nails gleaming like new moons,
skin soft as morning prayers,
each toe a well-tended garden.

These feet remember gratitude,
how every step is a choice,
how the earth rises to meet us
only as mindfully as we descend.

They understand the poetry of care:
that to tend to what carries us
is to honor where we're going,
and how we choose to arrive.
In their quiet radiance,
these feet betray their keeper's heart—
one who knows that life, like lotion,
must be worked in slowly, with purpose.

For what are feet but daily journals?
Recording each pause and sprint,
each dance and trudge,
each moment we chose to stand our ground.

Some read palms for fortune,
but I read feet for truth:
show me how you honor your foundation,
and I'll show you how you build your days.

In their well-moisturized wisdom,
they reveal an ancient truth:

that those who tend to life's smallest details
are dancing to rhythms others cannot hear.

Radiant Faces of Radiant Souls

Soul light seeps through skin
Beauty blooms from within

Glimmer eye shadows can't capture
The sparkle in joyful eyes

Heart writes on the face
Bitter thoughts etch lines
No cream can smooth away pain
Peace smooths from within

Watch how children glow
Before they learn to mirror—
Pure soul shining through

Joy cracks through facades
Like sunbeams through storm clouds break
True beauty escapes

Radiance flows up
From wells of inner stillness

"The Great Banana Bread Conspiracy"

Oh spotty banana, you temptress in brown,
Beckoning with promises of bread renown.
"This time," I declare, with conviction so bold,
"You'll be transformed before you grow mold!"

Ten years of intentions, all perfectly ripe,
Recipe bookmarked, everything's right!
The walnuts are waiting, the flour's on stand-by,
While bananas turn black and silently sigh.

"Tomorrow," I whisper, as spots multiply,
"You'll be a loaf that would make grandma cry!"
But tomorrow comes with its usual flair,
And my banana bread castle's still built in air.
From yellow to brown to mysterious black,
They've watched my ambition slowly slack.
These fruit basket martyrs, they've seen it before,

Their destiny's trash, not oven door.

A decade of dreams in perpetual pause,
Ten minutes too long, for reasons... because...
While Pinterest shows loaves all golden and proud,
My bananas join ancestors in compost crowd.

The walnuts are laughing, the mixing bowl weeps,
As another batch joins the "maybe next week"s.
Oh professional procrastination station!
Where banana bread's still in preparation.

Perhaps, in another decade or two,
I'll finally do what I've sworn I would do.
But for now, dear bananas, please understand—
You're not really bread, you're just my life's plan!

P.S. The fruit flies send their regards.

"Sisters Across Lifetimes"

Chrysanthemum meets Xewali in morning light,
Two gardens intertwining across ancient seas.
Your children's laughter echoes mine,
Three plus three, like stars reflecting in my very own Jur Pukhuri. [twin ponds]
In your tea ceremony, I see my grandmother's naam ghor,
Sacred moments braided like silk with cotton,
Our hands sharing stories older than continents,
Older than names, older than time itself.

Remember when we painted together?
Your brush spoke in Zen,
Mine answered in Madhubani,
Yet somehow they sang the same song.

Did we meet first under cherry blossoms,
Or beside a sacred Ganges bend?
Perhaps we taught each other art

In temples lost to time's soft veil.

Between Kyoto and Guwahati,
Our souls dance an ancient rhythm,
Teaching our children the art of seeing
beauty
In both rising sun and evening raga.

Some say oceans divide,
But we know better—
Water carries memories of old promises:
"I'll find you again, sister of my soul."

In every birth, a different garden,
But always the same flowering of love,
Our paths merging like brush strokes
In the cosmic painting of belonging.

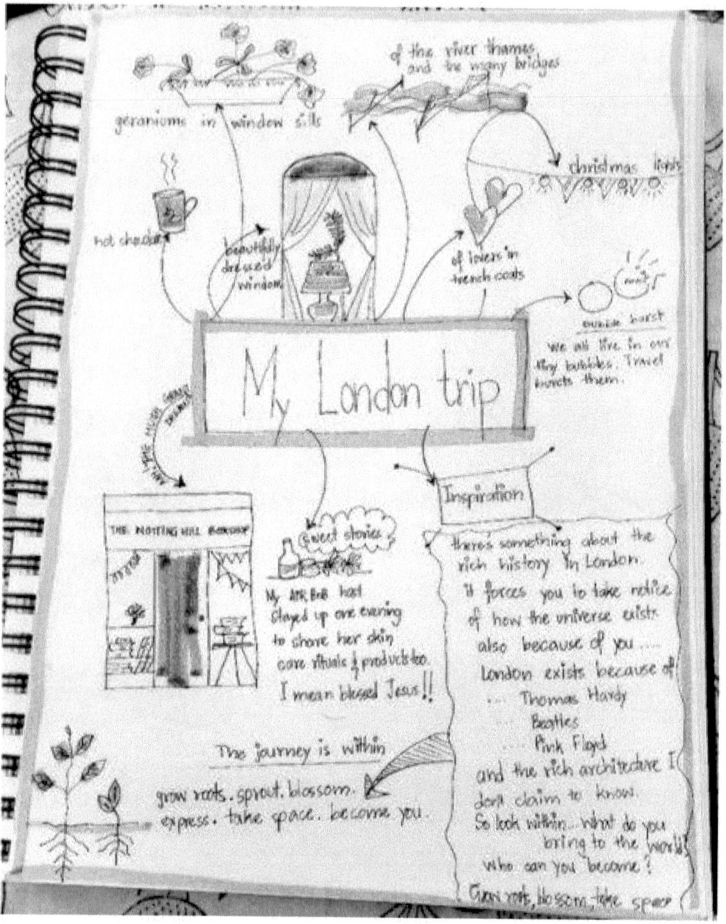
geraniums in window sills
of the river thames and the many bridges
christmas lights
hot chocolate
beautifully dressed window
of lovers in trench coats
bubble burst
we all live in our tiny bubbles. Travel bursts them.
My London trip
THE NOTTING HILL BOOKSHOP
sweet stories
My AIR BnB host stayed up one evening to share her skin care rituals & products too. I mean blessed Jesus!!
Inspiration
there's something about the rich history in London.
It forces you to take notice of how the universe exists also because of you....
London exists because of
... Thomas Hardy
... Beatles
.... Pink Floyd
and the rich architecture I don't claim to know.
So look within... what do you bring to the world?
Who can you become?
Grow roots, blossom, take space
The journey is within
grow roots. sprout. blossom.
express. take space. become you.

"London's Love Letters"

In the Blue Bookshop on Portobello,
Time forgets to tick,
Stories spill from weathered spines,
While antique hunters click past on
cobblestones.

Farmers' market mornings taste of
Earth-sweet strawberries and crusty
sourdough,
Where accents blend like tea leaves—
Cockney, Bengali, Jamaican, all London's
own.

Kensington's gardens hold secrets
Of children who never grew old,
Peter Pan playing hide and seek
Between ancient oaks and new dreams.

There's magic in the Mews,
Those hidden lanes of yesterday,
Where horses once clip-clopped past
Now hold homes like jewel boxes.

Ah, the writers' walls speak—
Hardy's thoughts still echo here,
Bowie's Brixton heart beats on,
Each blue plaque a portal to genius.

Piccadilly never sleeps,
Neon memories dance in puddles,
While somewhere in a quiet café
Off Abbey Road, stories brew in silence.

Hamleys' windows still enchant,
Five floors of childhood wonder,
Where even grown-up eyes sparkle
At dancing bears and flying things.

Trafalgar's pigeons plot their course
Between art and history,
While beneath museum arches
Dinosaurs dream of stars.

In salad bars at lunch hour,
City suits and artists queue together,
Trading pounds for rocket leaves
And stories of their morning tube.

Paddington's platforms promise
Adventures wrapped in paper,

Like marmalade sandwiches
Saved for rainy day journeys.

London Mews at twilight whisper
Tales of then and now,
Where gaslight shadows dance with LED dreams
And every cobblestone knows your name.

This city holds its treasures
Not in grand displays,
But in quiet corners where
Memory meets moment,
And every wanderer finds their way home.

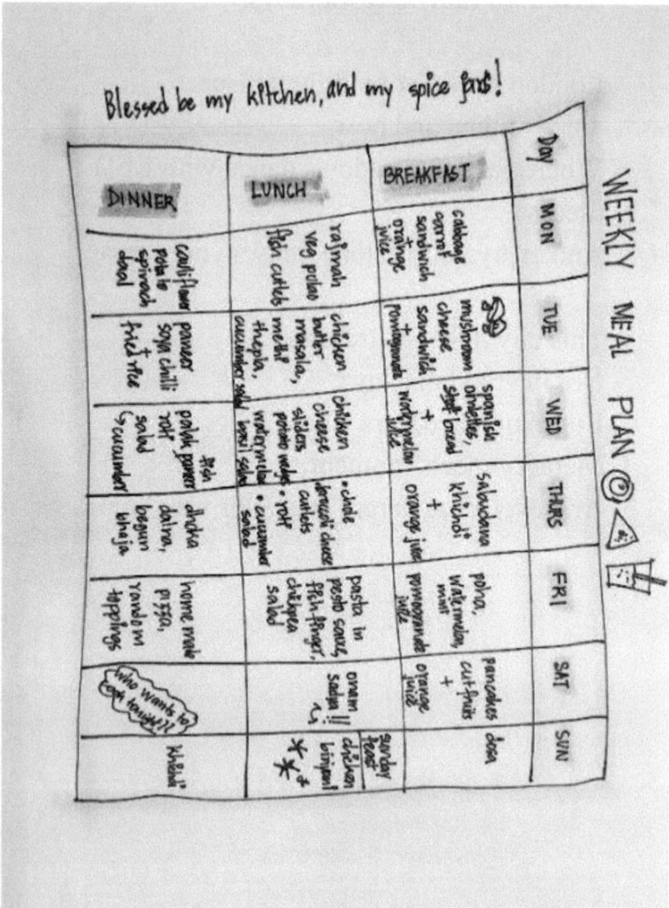
Blessed be my kitchen, and my spice jars!
WEEKLY MEAL PLAN
Day
MON
TUE
WED
THURS
FRI
SAT
SUN
BREAKFAST
LUNCH
DINNER

"The Currency of Care"

"Oh, I don't care what's for dinner," he
declares
(While secretly hoping for his mother's
special daal)
"Food is just fuel," says he with practiced air
(Yet sulks when dinner isn't quite up to par!)

"Your cooking takes too long," he sighs with
might
(As he spends three hours perfecting
spreadsheet height)
"Why such fuss over simple daily bread?"
(But heaven forbid if salad isn't freshly
spread!)

"I work so hard, you just are lost in your
writing and cook,"
(As if stirring pots requires no skill or book)
"My meetings are important, can't you see?"
(While managing three kids is apparently
free!)

"Your work's not measurable," he loves to say
(As if love and care come with a price display)
"Where's the ROI on all these homemade meals?"
(In that assessment, only mothers pass, wives and partners quite not!)

Poor man, so trapped in his corporate cage
Where emotions are weak and metrics engage
So busy proving his worth in gold
He's forgotten how to let joy unfold

"Real men don't cook," society taught him well
(Now he can't tell oregano from basil smell)
"Real men don't nurture," they said with pride
(Now he can't comfort his own inner child when it has cried)

Oh, what a price for patriarchy's crown!
One can't taste life, one can't slow down
Both trapped in roles we didn't choose
Both somehow destined to lose

But here's the joke that makes me smile:
While you count papers mile by mile,
I create memories, flavors, and care
Things no spreadsheet can compare!

So next time you say "I don't care what we eat,"
Remember this truth, both bitter and sweet:
In your rush to prove that time is gold,
You've missed the feast that life can hold!

P.S. The ROI on happiness?
Well, that's still pending in your assessment.

"To The Men Who Dare to Feel"

My heart aches for the boys you were,
Taught to swallow tears like bitter pills,
To transform tenderness into toughness,
Joy into metrics, love into bills.

Father, I saw how your hands longed
To plant roses instead of expectations,
How your heart sang when you cooked for us,
Despite the world's cold calculations.

Brother, how bravely you choose
To be present for your daughter's tears,
Breaking generational chains
That bound our fathers' fears.

To my friend who dares to dance,
Who paints his nails and bares his soul,
Who knows strength lives in gentleness—
You make this broken world more whole.

To my son discovering wonder,

May you never learn to dim your light,
Your laughter precious as morning dew,
Your softness fierce as night.

I see you all, fighting silent battles
Against "man up" and "boys don't cry,"
Choosing to nurture gardens of feeling
Under harsh patriarchal sky.

How heavy that armor must have been—
The constant proving, providing, pace,
The marathons of manufactured worth,
The fear of falling from false grace.

But oh, how beautiful you are
When you let that armor fall,
When you cook with unhurried joy,
When you answer connection's call.

I celebrate your quiet revolutions:
The bedtime stories tenderly read,
The tears shed at beauty's touch,
The gentle ways you choose to lead.

To every man who dares to pause,
Who trades status for presence true,
Who chooses love over legacy—

This poem is my thank you.

For every moment you resist
The world's demand to harden, hide,
You create space for others' healing,
Let tenderness and strength reside.

In your defiance of cold metrics,
Your embrace of heart and art,
You free not just yourselves, but all—
This is how healing starts.
To all the men I deeply love,
Who walk this path with grace:
Your courage to remain tender
Makes this world a softer place.

Beautiful Constraints

what is this life. full of care
we have no time to stand and stare
no time to turn at Beauty's glance,
And watch her feet, how they can dance.
No time to wait till her mouth can,
Enrich the smile that her eyes began.

"CEO of Human Potential"

Between 2 AM feedings and quantum physics lessons,
We birth not just bodies, but neural networks,
Each synapse a future market trend,
Each question an untapped opportunity.

Your startup incubates in Silicon Valley?
I incubate wonder in a child's eyes—
My ROI measured in light-bulb moments,
In questions that crack universes open.

Board meetings? I hold them cross-legged on floors,
Where Miyazaki meets mitochondria,
Where Kafka's metamorphosis tangos with caterpillars,
And Darwin whispers through backyard expeditions.

My strategic planning spans generations,
Each bedtime story, a seed round of imagination,

Each "why?" a potential unicorn of
innovation,
Each meltdown, a lesson in crisis
management.

Your market research? I study soul patterns,
Map the topography of growing minds,
Scale mountains of possibility daily,
Between lunch boxes and life's meaning.

My venture capital? Time, infinite patience,
Investing in moments when eyes spark with
knowing,
When Fibonacci spirals appear in shell
collections,
When double slits split light and certainty.

You disrupt markets?
I disrupt conditioning.
You scale platforms?
I scale human consciousness.

Mother as CEO,
Running Earth's most vital incubator,
Each child a startup of infinite potential,
Each day a new round of funding the future.

The privilege? Oh, the privilege—
To relearn wonder through fresh eyes,
To birth not just beings but beginnings,
To steward stardust into story.

So, tell me again about your important meetings,
While I'm here engineering humanity's next leap,
One curious question at a time,
One soul-spark into flame.

For what is motherhood but the ultimate venture—
Into the human heart, the cosmic mind,
Each child, a universe of possibilities,
Each mother, an architect of tomorrow.

We don't just raise children,
We raise the stakes of human potential.
We don't just manage homes,
We manage humanity's next iteration.

And in return? We get to be students again,
Learning life anew through their eyes,
Our dividends paid in daily revelations,
Our success measured in awakened souls.

This is not just parenting—
This is paradigm-shifting.
This is not just motherhood—
This is the future taking flight.

Dancing in Morning Light

A giant spoon rests in delight,
Bearing its cherry red and round
Above Minneapolis' hallowed ground.
A whimsical sight in steel and shine,
Where art and play intertwine,
Like a dessert for giants free—
The Spoonbridge stands for all to see.
In summer's warmth or winter's white,
This sculptured spoon brings pure delight,
A testament to joy unfurled
In this corner of the modern world.

The Last Sunday of 2024: Museum of Art and Photography, Bangalore

In the quiet halls of MAP, where time slows down,
December's last breath whispers through glass cases
and climate-controlled histories.
I stand before an 18th-century peacock bust,
carved from someone's patience,
each bead with multiple inceptions.

Who were those hands?
What heartbeat beneath the chisel
that could see so deeply into wood,
that could wait so long
for beauty to emerge?

They must have known something we've forgotten—
the holy ritual of staying still,
of letting time pool around the ankles
like evening shadows.

My phone buzzes in my pocket.
(I check it, of course I do)
Three notifications, two emails,
one AI-generated masterpiece
born in the time it takes to blink.

The peacock watches me,
its wooden eye holding centuries
of undivided attention.

I think about my morning coffee,
how I scroll through art like weather,
tapping, swiping, double-tapping praise,
my thumb, a blind pilgrim
searching for sanctuary.

Beauty is my religion, I whisper to the
peacock.
But what kind of devotee am I,
with my fractured prayers,
my half-hearted meditation,
my plastic offerings of partial presence?

The artisan who carved you
must have lived in you,
breathed with you,

dreamed you into being.
Each morning, they chose to return
to your slow becoming.

I want to learn this patience again,
to kneel at the altar of detail,
to let beauty work its slow miracle
through my restless hands.

But already my mind skips ahead,
like a stone across water,
touching down briefly
before moving on.

The peacock keeps its vigil,
a testament to what we once could see
when we gave ourselves permission
to look deeply,
to stay,
to witness.

Going on a Bear Hunt Through Streets Once Still

Down empty streets where silence reigned
A mother and her crew remained
Three boys, a dog, and one brave soul
Who never let the darkness take its toll

At nine, ten, eleven years
Her sons watched as magic appears
For Mama wasn't just their guide
But fellow adventurer by their side

With arms spread wide, she'd chase the wind
Her laughter with their giggles twinned
"Adventure calls!" she'd daily cry
As neighbors watched her spirit fly

No bear too fierce, no path too long
Her heart beat to childhood's song
Dancing through the quiet days
Leading them through nature's maze

The dog would bark, the boys would leap
Through puddles shallow, puddles deep

And she, their mother, led the way
Finding wonder day by day

When others saw the world grow small
She taught them how to stand up tall
For in her heart, she'd kept alive
The child who helped them all survive

Through lockdown's strange and solemn days
She showed them all the playful ways
To turn their walks into a quest
Where imagination did the rest

Years may pass, the boys may grow
But they'll remember what they know:
Their mother's spirit, wild and free
Teaching them how life should be.

The Stories My Earrings Tell

On my vintage stand of brass and dreams,
They catch the light in scattered gleams—
Each pair a chapter, each hook a verse,
Of stories I choose to reminisce.

Blue butterflies dance from my ears to sky,
Reminding me how I learned to fly.
Golden lotuses, ancient and wise,
Speak of connections that I deeply prize.

Here, pressed flowers in amber sealed,
Whisper secrets of summer fields.
Some hug close, like sister's love—
The pair she gave when push came shove.

Modern pieces, clean and spare,
Tell of days I learned to dare.
While aita's thurias, heavy with tales,
Ring with uplifting stories that never fail.

My best friend knew—that silver pair
With the vibrant beads so rare,
Matches the light she sees in me

When I forget what others see.

And oh, these new ones, fresh with hope,
Each one chosen by him who spoke
Love in metals, gems, and gold,
Adding stories yet untold.

They dangle like wind chimes in my soul,
Some pieces missing, yet I'm whole.
Each morning as I choose to wear
A piece of life caught hanging there,

I see myself in mirrored shine,
In curves of metal, crystals fine.
My collection grows like rings in trees,
Each pair, a self I chose to be.

For in these tiny works of art,
I wear my stories near my heart,
And when they catch the morning light,
My soul's shine makes them twice as bright.

Mirror, Mirror—Delight Me!

She stands before the mirror, not searching for flaws but finding constellations in her own universe. Her fingers trace the gentle slopes of her face, not perfect by magazine standards, but perfect in its authenticity. The mirror isn't her judge today; it's her confidant, her celebration.

That smile—oh, that smile—it starts in her eyes before it even reaches her lips. It's like watching a sunrise in slow motion, the way it spreads across her face, lighting up each imperfection until they become beauty marks in their own right. Her teeth aren't piano-key straight, but when she grins, they create a symphony of joy that she conducts with her laughter.

On this rainy afternoon, while others huddle under umbrellas and curse the weather, she's creating her own sunshine. The brush glides through her hair—not to tame it, but to feel its wild strength. The lip gloss isn't armor; it's pure pleasure, catching light like dewdrops on morning petals. She's not preparing to face the world; she's savoring her own company.

Her eyes hold stories that no filter could capture—little creases at the corners from years of genuine laughter, a spark of mischief that dances just beneath the surface. There's something magical about the way her face transforms when she's truly delighted, as if her soul is too bright to be contained beneath her skin.

In this moment, before the mirror, she's both artist and masterpiece, observer and observed. She doesn't need the validation of passing glances or hollow compliments. Her beauty isn't a performance—it's a private joy, a secret garden where she blooms for no one but herself.

Home as an Allegory of the Mind: The Tidying Paradox

Marie Kondo smiles from dusty shelves,
Between unfolded laundry piles that mock themselves.
"Your space reflects your mind," the monk book states,
While yesterday's dishes patiently wait.

She downloads apps to track her mess,
Buys containers to contain her stress.
Then screams, "Your rooms are chaos, kids!"
While her own drawer won't shut its lid.

The books pile up like gentle blame:
"Declutter life! Reclaim your frame!"
But wisdom drowns in coffee rings,
On self-help books of tidier things.

Xuwoni

Xuwoni, our enchanting home,
Built with patience and prayer,
Like a bird weaving its nest—
One twig, one dream at a time,
Until charm and peace
Find their perfect resting place
In this space, we call our own.

The Queen of Good Intentions

Every New Year's Eve, she makes her solemn vow,
"This year I'll be organized!" (She's said this till now).
With Pinterest boards bursting and schedules so neat,
Her plans are perfection, her systems complete!

"Monday's for rugs, and Tuesday's for towels,
Wednesday's for linens!" she cheerfully howls.
"Saturday morning, the plants get their drink!"
But chaos erupts faster than she can think.

Three homes she's moved to, each time with a cry:
"No junk this time!" (Oh, what a beautiful lie!)
Boxes still packed from two moves ago,

What's in them? Well, honey, we'll never quite know!

Her teenager rolls eyes at mom's latest scheme,
"Remember the craft room? Your upcycling dream?"
Half-painted mason jars crowd every spare space,
While Pinterest projects mock her with grace.

That cardboard collection she swears she'll reuse,
Those fabric scraps waiting to become something new,
The wine corks she's saving (for what? Who can tell?)
And organizing boxes... still wrapped, can't you smell?

In drawers and in cupboards, behind every door,
Lie good intentions scattered all over the floor.
Her house isn't messy, she'll firmly insist,

"It's just that my projects are... works in progress!"

So here's to our hero, still making her lists,
Still downloading apps that swear organization exists.
While Marie Kondo sparks joy with minimal flair,
Our friend's sparking chaos with unmatched love and care!

P.S. She's just made a new resolution today,
To sort through the mess (but first, let's hit "Save"
On twelve more Pinterest boards of storage solutions)
While last year's planners join the clutter's revolution!

Tangled Up in Time

Like a rolling stone from Guwahati's hills,
She once dreamed wild beneath mango
trees,
While he traced their paths through times
that would be,
Two dreamers dancing in the endless rain.

Manhattan's shelter of steel embraced him,
While she stayed behind, blowin' in the
wind
Of domestic shores—lunch boxes, school
runs,
Her tambourine fading to kitchen chimes.

Through WhatsApp pixels, he sends her
signs:
"Remember when we were forever young?"
Songs like compass points marking her way
back:
Girl from the North Country, still fierce, still
free.

When the weight of ladles dims her fire,
He shares Mr. Tambourine Man to remind
How they once chased melody through midnight,
Before societal roles stole more time from her.

Shelter from the Storm lights up her screen
As she stirs another pot of her son's favourite chicken curry,
His message: "You're still that knockin' on heaven's door,
Behind those grocery lists and folded clothes."

Between Tangled Up in Blue memories
And Simple Twist of Fate that pulled them far,
Their friendship holds her compass true to north,
Each Dylan verse, a breadcrumb home to self.

Now she hums Forever Young while cooking,
Finding rhythm in routine's disguise,
Remembering the girl who once knew how

To dream beyond the Times They Are A-Changin'.

Some of my favourite things
Beautiful Plants
Freshly baked
beauty care
Beautiful Food
aroma
chokers
Centre-piece
cut flowers
dream catcher

What Can You Say About a Girl

What can you say about a girl who read Ayn
Rand and listened to Alanis Morissette,
much before the world around her could
spell the same?
Who knew addiction was just love seeking
warmth in winter's gloom?

Her wisdom preceded Maté's trauma and
compassionate inquiry, understanding hearts
that bled
Into needles and powder, searching for
belonging in chemical illusions.

What can you say about her Valentine
wishes?
No roses or chocolates would do—
She wanted Cobain's final words printed,
downloaded from World Wide Web,
In an era when modems still had to dial up,
and stay connected only for a moment or
two.

Her crown was her rebellion:
Shorn locks and metal multiplicities in cartilage,
Sometimes stripped to skin like a monk's declaration,
Carrying mystery like a torch in her stride.

What can you say about her sonic universe?
Anjan Dutta's urban poetry melted into AC DC's thunder,
Baul mystics danced with Mercury's rhapsody,
While Tagore's verses were her natural eloquence in any situation.

What can you say about her defiance of papers and rings?
She'd laugh at the notion of love requiring witnesses,
"Hearts don't need contracts," she'd declare,
"They either belong or they don't."

What can you say about this girl?
She was fire-wearing skin,
Magic dressed in kurtas from Sarojini,
A revolution wrapped in riddles.

Suprabhatam Meets Soundgarden

She moshed to Pearl Jam in Guwahati rain,
While he woke to Venkatesa's holy strain.
Her torn denims scandalized Chennai's
streets;
His aunts fainted at her floral skirt pleats.

In Meenakshi temple, he folded hands,
While she dreamed of underground rock
bands.
Her breakfast: eggs with hollandaise sauce,
His morning idli left her at a loss.

She'd grown up with boys as equals, friends,
He'd look away when girl-talk descends.
Her mekhela swayed at metal gigs;
His world was jasmine, silk, and traditional
digs.

At A2B, she'd tease his filter coffee flame,
"But have you tried cold brew?" (Oh, the
shame!)
He'd silently admire her fearless speech,
While clutching his privacy like a breach.

Two worlds apart like rasam and masor tenga,
Yet love brewed stronger than filter kaapi and orthodox Assam tea.
She taught him rock; he taught her Carnatic,
Their love story—perfectly dramatic.

North-East fire meets Tamil reserve,
A recipe that shouldn't work, but does with verve.

The Mathematical Mother

Her teens roll their eyes when she explains
How love grows like Fibonacci's gains.
"Mom, it's just homework," they protest in vain,
While she draws spirals, again and again.

At parent-teacher meetings, she'll digress
About Schrödinger's cat and quantum mess.
"Your son's missing classes," the teacher states,
"But isn't uncertainty just so great?"

Helping with chemistry homework means
Reciting the periodic table in her dreams.
"Titanium's not just a David Guetta song!
It's atomic number 22—sing along!"

Trigonometry brings her special joy,
"Sin, cos, tan," she tells her annoyed boys,
"Are like life's ups and downs, you see?"
They groan, "Mom, it's just geometry!"

She signs up for Khan Academy's course,
"To help with homework," she claims, of course.
But late at night, she's solving proofs,
While teenage snores echo from their rooms.

Her WhatsApp status: "π r^2 above,
Is like the circle of mother's love."
The boys have blocked her, truth be told,
But math won't let this geek grow old.

The Pedagogically Perfect Parent

Montessori says "A place for all!"
While Legos migrate down the hall.
"Work mats define your space," books
preach,
As toys spread faster than they teach.

Steiner whispers "Find your rhythm!"
(Between Netflix and tantrums with them).
"Everything must have a purpose here" –
Tell that to seventeen stuffed bears.

Reggio preaches "Follow their lead!"
(To chaos at lightning speed).
"Child-led learning!" experts say,
As markers decorate the way.

Each night she googles "parenting fails,"
While pulling hair and growing pale.
"I'm surely ruining them!" she cries,
Until sleep brings peaceful lies.

Yet somehow they've turned out fine,
Despite her pedagogic design.
The universe knew what it meant,
When choosing this imperfect parent.

The Art of Being Swetha

In the gentle rhythm of her hands,
Washing ceramic bowls with mindful grace,
Lives beauty in its purest form—
Each plate a canvas of everyday art.

Empty frames adorn her walls,
Their absence more profound than presence,
Teaching us that spaces between
Hold beauty yet to come.

Her home speaks in whispers
Of muted greys and gentle beige,
Where chaos finds order
Without losing its soul.

Watch her arrange fallen leaves
In crystal bowls with quiet precision,
Making poetry from autumn's debris,
Finding music in mundane moments.
Even the sharp edges of life
Grow soft within her touch,
Like morning light diffused
Through her gossamer curtains.

She teaches us, without words,
That beauty dwells in process,
In half-finished dreams and
Perfectly imperfect moments.

Her life—an unfinished sculpture,
Each day a gentle chisel stroke,
Showing us how grace lives
In the spaces still becoming.

Be Careful What You Wish For

I wished for brilliance, creativity divine,
A child like Calvin from the comic strip's line.
The universe listened, oh what a jest—
Now my second-born puts sanity to test!

The palak paneer's on the ceiling today,
"A gravity experiment gone astray!"
Rotis hidden in the crystal display,
"They needed a vacation, they told me, okay?"

The orange juice vanished? Check the plants,
"They were thirsty!" comes his casual grants.
While neighbors learn shapes of morning poo,
Through window-shouted stories, loud and true.

Dead bugs in jars line his shelf with pride,
"T-Rex's breakfast!" he happily confides.
The free-range eggs? Don't bother to look,
They're "incubating dinosaurs" in his pop-up book.

Living with genius isn't what it seems,
When genius comes with six-year-old dreams.
But then he hugs me, eyes bright as the stars,
"Mamma, I love you more than where numbers end."

Not Quite Tea Parties

She dreamed of ribbons, lace, and tea,
Instead got wrestling times three.
No dolls in sight, no pink tulle swirls,
Just boys, their tractors and concrete mixers
and no mention of any girls.

Their weapon of choice? The silent kind,
That leaves victims gasping far behind.
"He dutch-ovened my room!" one cries,
While another plots his fart-filled lies.

The eldest guards his deadly secret,
Till sibling wars make him leak it:
"Post-kebab, he's lethal gas!
Keep your sleepovers in hazmat!"

"Five kilometers!" middle one swears,
"That's how far his stench-cloud bears!"
The youngest adds with expert flair,
"NASA tracks it through the air!"

No tea parties grace her maternal scene,
Just boys comparing whose is more obscene.

While somewhere in her closet lies
A dress with ribbons, small in size.

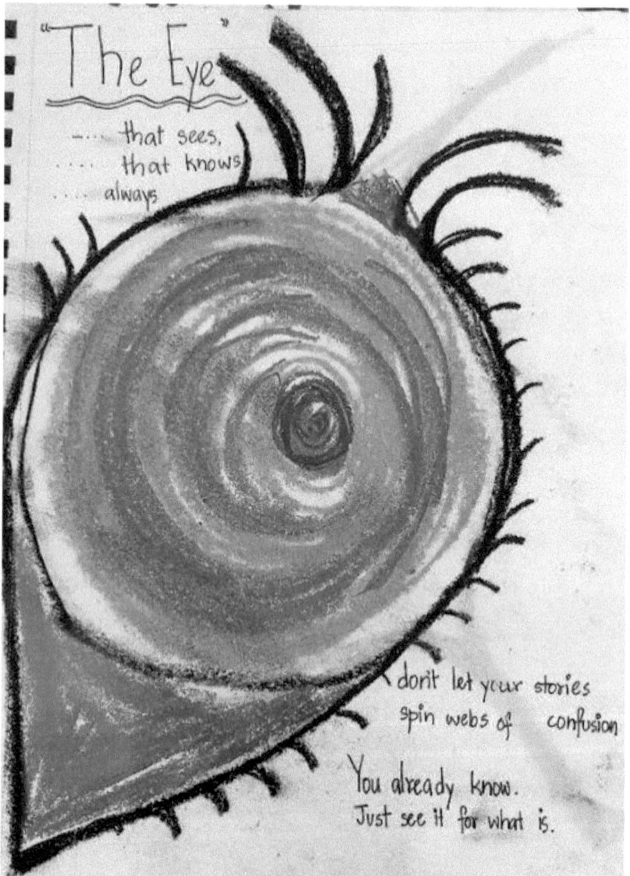
"The Eye"
...that sees,
....that knows
....always
don't let your stories
spin webs of confusion
You already know.
Just see it for what is.

The Good Girl's Lament

Pastels and pleats, neat cursive on the
page—
I built this prison one gold star at a time,
Each "well done, dear" another gleaming
cage,
Each perfect score, a rung I had to climb.

The neighborhood watched as I played my
part:
Their model daughter, poised in powder
blue,
While somewhere deep within my restless
heart,
A wildness stirred that no one ever knew.

"Look at her manners, look how sweet she
speaks!"
They'd whisper as I passed their garden
gates.
I smiled and nodded, felt my spirit leak
Through cracks between the bars I helped
create.

Small town, small dreams, they carved me to their needs—
A porcelain doll upon their mantlepiece,
Until my edges blurred, and who indeed
Was left of me beneath this masterpiece?
Lorde's words echo through my hollow frame:
"Define yourself, or others eat you whole."
Too late I saw the truth of what became:
A feast of self, served on a perfect scroll.

Devoured alive by others' fantasies,
Their hunger shaped me into what they'd praise.
Now middle-aged, I touch my boundaries
And feel the phantom weight of wasted days.

But deep within these bones, a truth remains,
Unvarnished, raw, and refusing to fade:
The parts I buried underneath the strain
Of being good—they never went away.

So, let me now unlearn this perfect pose,
Embrace the wild creature in my core.

The shame that binds—I'll shed it like old clothes,
And dance unbound, as never danced before.

For in this body lives a feral grace,
That never needed polish, never asked
For permission just to take up space—
The real girl behind the good girl's mask.

Raised on Equal Rights

They said, "Be strong, be fierce, be equal!"
Mother's battle cry echoes through decades of struggle
Her textbooks were her rebellion, her degree her victory march
"The world is yours now, daughter—seize it!"

So, I learned to change tires in business suits
Drove forklifts while quoting Woolf
Grunge music and red lipstick became my war paint
Until father's warning cut through:
"Not too visible, not too loud, not too much"

Equal enough to work, but not to shine
Independent enough to survive, but not to thrive
A paradox wrapped in progress
Packaged as liberation

I drag my own boxes up three flights of stairs

Because I can, because I should, because I must
File my taxes, fix the leak, feed the kids
Independence becomes a self-imposed exile

Years pile up like moving boxes
Each one labeled "I can do it myself"
Until my strength becomes my prison
And solitude morphs into solitary confinement

Now at forty, I count accomplishments like battle scars
Each "I did it alone" a badge of honor
That weighs heavy like chain mail
In the quiet moments between being strong
And being human

Mother never told me liberation could be lonely
That equality didn't mean doing everything
Just the right to choose what to do
Now I wonder—did we confuse
Independence with isolation? And equality with being identical?

The feminist dream turned solitary scheme
As I sit in my self-made fortress
Built from equal opportunities
And missed connections
Wondering if being strong
Meant I had to be alone.

Cosmic Choreography

It wasn't chance that made us two—
you, following my footsteps like a shadow
but never quite in them.
The universe knew what it was doing
when it made me first, you second,
daughters in duplicate, yet distinct.

Our shared wardrobe was more than cloth:
borrowed sweaters carrying stories,
hand-me-downs bearing whispered histories.
In convent corridors, we watched the rich
girls shine
in branded glory while we wore
middle-class dreams stitched with mother's
care.
But we had what they didn't—
a mirror soul to reflect our worth.

You were my midnight consultant
before every test, every presentation,
my emergency fashion advisor,
my partner in winter picnic preparations.
When Durga Puja came,

we'd traverse the markets like explorers,
each purchase a joint venture,
each decision a duet.

Some secrets we carried together
were heavier than schoolbags—
family shadows we learned to fold
and tuck away, knowing
that shared burdens grow lighter,
like darkness split between two hearts.

The years spun gold from simple things:
matching bangles jingling at festivals,
two cups of tea in morning light,
your laughter echoing mine
in perfect harmony.
Now, I understand why stars come in
clusters—
they're brighter together,
like sisters meant to light each other's way.

Looking back, I see the poetry
in our parallel lives:
how your presence multiplied my world,
how my steps carved paths for yours,
how we built a symphony
from borrowed clothes and shared sorrows,

from festival lights and midnight whispers.
This was always meant to be—
this dance of two daughters,
this sisterhood of souls.

Winter Mornings in Guwahati

In the fog of winter mornings,
We emerged like a strange sight—
You, in your worn eri kurta,
Threading through narrow lanes,
Your muffler a beacon of mismatched hues,
Handmade with love across seasons.

The Bajaj scooter, our faithful companion,
Carried dreams wrapped in morning chill,
From Dighalipukhiripar to Beltola,
Each turn marking another quest
For the excellence you understood,
The only language we shared.

You never knew my favorite colors,
Or the whispers of my heart,
But you knew this—
The weight of ambition,
The roads that led to possibility,
The mathematics of hope.

Friends would spot us from afar,
That peculiar pair on wheels:
A father in his garish winter armor,
And his daughter, clutching books and dreams—
"There she goes," they'd say,
"With her foolish dream-keeper."

Now I know why those winters shine so bright
In memory's tepid glow—
Not for the conversations we never had,
Or the homework you couldn't help with,
But for those silent morning rides,
When love wore tacky colors
And drove a scooter through the mist,
Believing in something
It could barely understand.

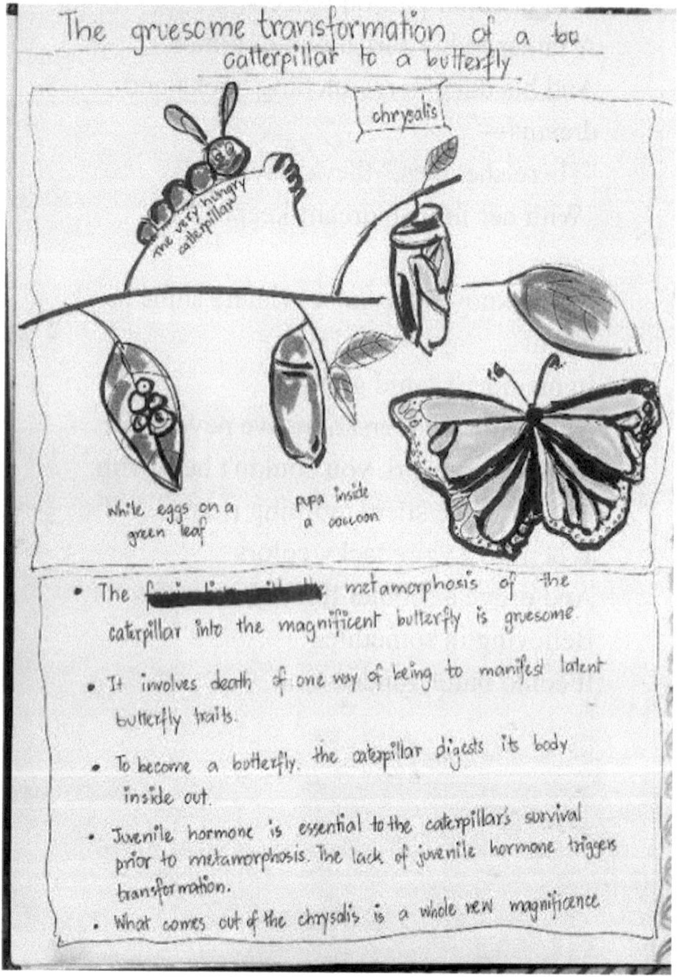
The gruesome transformation of a bo
catterpillar to a butterfly
chrysalis
The very hungry caterpillar
white eggs on a green leaf
pupa inside a cocoon
• The metamorphosis of the caterpillar into the magnificent butterfly is gruesome
• It involves death of one way of being to manifest latent butterfly traits.
• To become a butterfly, the caterpillar digests its body inside out.
• Juvenile hormone is essential to the caterpillar's survival prior to metamorphosis. The lack of juvenile hormone triggers transformation.
• What comes out of the chrysalis is a whole new magnificence

The Alchemy of Shame

Once, I was bronze and bold,
Like that defiant girl on Wall Street—
Hands on hips, chin raised high,
Wind in my hair, fear nowhere in sight.

Then came the whispers,
Like poison in morning tea:
"Your body is a betrayal,"
"Your blood is a curse,"
"Your existence—a debt to be paid
In dishes, diapers, and designated silence."

They wrapped me in shame
Like a sari of shadows,
Each fold a lesson in submission:
"Stand smaller,"
"Speak softer,"
"Serve better."

Ancient stories became handcuffs:
"Woman was made from man's rib,"
They said, as if my bones
Were borrowed property,

As if my breath was stolen air,
As if my dreams were crimes.

My spirit—once a wildfire—
Became smoke in their hands.
Three decades of darkness,
Carrying guilt like inherited jewelry,
Wearing shame like a second-skin
Until it felt like my own face.

But now I see—
I was never the broken one.
I was just a vessel they poured their fear into,
A crucible for their ancient terrors:
What if women walked unburdened?
What if girls never learned to apologize for their light?

The shame was never mine—
I was just its alchemist,
Transforming their lead into my gold,
Their fear into my freedom.
Let me shed this borrowed skin,
This hand-me-down guilt.

Watch me rise,

Not a pawn but a player,
Not a victim but a vessel
For transformation.
The society that feared my fire
Will witness its own reflection
In my unleashed flame.

For if one woman stands unashamed,
A thousand chains begin to rust.
If one girl reclaims her power,
A thousand cages start to crack.
I am not collateral damage—
I am the catalyst for change.

The Unfilled Cup

Look at them—these mothers
With adult bones but child hearts,
Walking paradoxes of giving
From wells run dry generations ago.
Their hands shake as they pour
What they never received.

The maiden stage—
Nature's sacred preparation,
A time meant for filling,
For learning the art of receiving
Before the giving begins.
But who teaches a starving heart to feast?

See how they stumble,
These grown women with toddler tears
Trapped beneath their skin,
Their nervous systems still singing
Songs of ancient abandonment,
While society demands they mother.

They were meant to be:
Treasured before treasuring,

Held before holding,
Seen before seeing,
Loved before loving—
This is the natural order.

Instead, they are:
Stripped of softness,
Racing through corridors of competition,
Contorting to impossible standards,
Their bodies battlegrounds
For beauty's brutal war.

And then we wonder—
Why children wake crying,
Why homes feel hollow,
Why love comes out twisted
Like water through rusted pipes,
Why chaos breeds chaos.

The solution lies
In nature's wisdom:
Let the maiden receive
Until her cup overflows,
Until her laughter rings true,
Until her wounds turn to wisdom.

For a mother can only give

What once filled her own cup—
Joy begets joy,
Wholeness creates wholeness,
Love multiplies love,
This is the mathematics of healing.

So let us protect our maidens,
Guard their right to grow slow,
To be awkward and unsure,
To need and receive,
To fill their wells deep
Before life asks them to pour.

For in saving the maiden,
We save the mother,
And in saving the mother,
We save the world—
One full cup at a time,
One healed heart at a time.

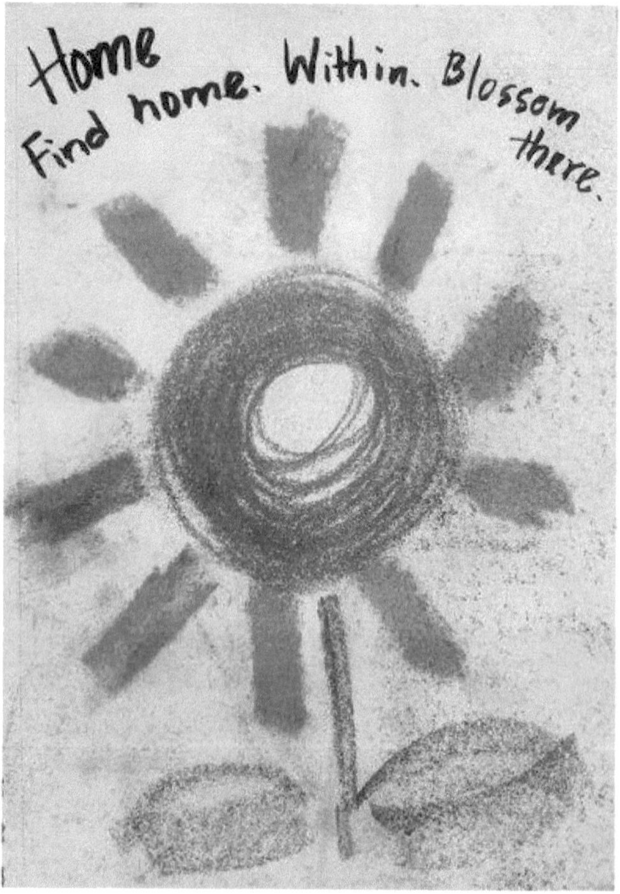
Home
Find home. Within. Blossom there.

The Sacred Art of Re-Parenting

They did what they knew—
Our parents, those wounded healers,
Passing down their unfinished stories
Like inherited jewelry, across generations,
Tarnished but precious still.

Now we stand here,
Adults with child-hearts,
Finally holding the keys
To our own healing:
Books, therapists, wisdom-keepers,
Tools they never had.

The greatest gift we can give ourselves:
To parent our inner children
With the tenderness they missed,
To whisper "I see you"
To those forgotten parts,
To hold space for ancient tears.

What would it feel like
To inhabit each moment fully?

To feel sunlight without shadows of the past,
To laugh without checking over our
shoulder,
To love without armor?

This is our sacred responsibility—
Not a burden, but a blessing,
To complete the incomplete circles,
To tend our internal gardens,
To choose presence over patterns.

For in healing ourselves,
We heal seven generations back
And seven forward.
This is how we transform
From wounded to whole,
One conscious breath at a time.

Rish's 11th Birthday party planning
Noodles
sandwiches
sliders
BOW-TIE PASTA

In the Chamber of Motherhood

I stand before my mirror, not to see
The silver threading through my patient hair,
But glimpse the queen I daily strive to be—
For noble princes need a sovereign's care.

My three young knights, still wrestling in the sun,
Must learn to wield both tenderness and might.
The path to princely wisdom has begun
Within my own quest for the crown of light.

Each morning as I don my unseen crown,
I weave for them a tapestry of grace:
In scripture's wisdom, stories of renown,
In myths that time itself cannot erase.

For how can I implore them to be kind
If anger rules my own untamed domain?
How to teach them beauty of the heart and mind
If I let chaos in my kingdom reign?

So, daily do I polish my own soul,
Let radiance illuminate my way,
For every mother bears this sacred role:
To live the virtue that her words convey.

My scepter is not gold but patient love,
My throne built not of ivory but time,
My kingdom's treasure stored in realms above,
Where character outweighs the paradigm.

Through them I see the future's gleaming face:
Three princes rising, strong yet gentle-souled,
Each bearing gifts of valor mixed with grace,
Their hearts pure silver in life's testing gold.

So, let me rise each dawn and choose again
To wear this crown of mindful majesty,
For only queens can raise these noble men
To heights of their divine capacity.

In them, I plant the seeds of reverence,
Of creativity's unfettered flight,

Of empathy's encompassing presence,
Of wisdom's clear, unwavering light.

The jewels I give them are not gems that
shine
But moments when I model what I teach:
When patience triumphs, when my thoughts
align
With higher purpose within my reach.

For in this sacred art of raising kings,
The truth emerges, luminous and clear:
The noblest gift a mother ever brings
Is being what she hopes her sons hold dear.

So, let me be the queen they need to see:
Resplendent, learned, purposeful and wise,
For in my sovereignty, they'll come to be
The noble princes I see in their eyes.

The Tale of Maya and Bono: A Tale of Two Streets

On Curley and Bride, two streets apart,
Lived Maya and Bono, soon to steal each other's heart.
She, a regal Lab with grace divine,
He, handsome and spirited, his eyes would shine.

Their human mamas, Pavithra and Kakoli,
Would arrange their meetings, oh so holy!
Paw dates in parks, beneath the trees,
Where love bloomed soft as summer's breeze.

Maya's dignity met Bono's charm,
Their connection strong, pure and warm.
Two souls united, destinies entwined,
A love so rare, one of a kind.

Then came January's morning light,
Bringing wonders, such a sight!
Eleven puppies, perfect and new,

Each one special, precious and true.

There's Ruskin, Luca, and playful Huggy,
Fredo and Olive, so sweet and snuggy.
Lily and Bella, with tails a-wag,
Maya Jr. and Zoey, making hearts lag.
Dear Kara racing across the floor,
And tiny Nemo, loved even more.

Forty-four paws now pitter-patter,
Eleven pairs of eyes now scatter
Joy and laughter everywhere they go,
A family's love continues to grow.

More than dogs and more than friends,
This tale of love never ends.
For Pavi and Kakoli, Maya and Bono too,
Created magic that binds hearts anew.

The universe in its infinite design,
Brought thirteen souls to intertwine.
Through whiskers, wagging tails, and paws,
Love found its way, just because.

Printed by Libri Plureos GmbH in Hamburg, Germany

9 789360 942397